Seymour

Pyramids & Mummies

SCHOLASTIC INC.

New York Toronto London Auckland Sydney
Mexico City New Delhi Hong Kong Buenos Aires

Front cover photograph: the Pyramid of Khufu and the Sphinx
Title page photograph: a Diorite statue of the Pharaoh Khafre

This book is dedicated to my son Michael.

Special thanks to reading consultant Dr. Linda B. Gambrell, Director, School of Education, Clemson University. Dr. Gambrell has served as President of the National Reading Conference and Board member of the International Reading Association.

Permission to use the following photographs is gratefully acknowledged:
front cover, pages 18–19: © Michele Burgess; title page: © Robert Partridge: The Ancient Egypt Picture Library; pages 2–3, 7, 8–9, 14–15, 16–17, 29: © Tor Eigeland; pages 4–5, 22–23, 40, back cover: © Kenneth Garrett; pages 10–11, 32–33: © Christine Osborne Pictures; pages 12–13, 34–35: © Eugene G. Schultz; pages 20–21: © Blaine Harrington; page 25: © Dan McCoy/Rainbow; page 27: © Boltin Picture Library; pages 30–31: © David Lawrence; pages 36–37: © Chuck Place Photography; pages 38–39: © Luxor Hotel Press Office.

ISBN 0-439-56094-2

Text copyright © 2003 by Seymour Simon. All rights reserved.
Published by Scholastic Inc., 557 Broadway, New York, NY 10012,
by arrangement with North-South Books, Inc. SCHOLASTIC and associated logos
are trademarks and/or registered trademarks of Scholastic Inc.

12 11 10 9 8 7 6 5 4 3 2   4 5 6 7 8 9/0

Printed in the U.S.A.   23

First Scholastic printing, January 2004

The early Egyptians built pyramids
nearly 5,000 years ago. They believed
their king, the pharaoh (FAIR-oh), was
a living god. Each pyramid was built
as a tomb for a pharaoh, to bring him
eternal life.

The Egyptians thought the pharaoh was descended from Re (RAY), the sun god. After the pharaoh died, his spirit returned to join the gods in the next world. But, if the pharaoh's body decayed, then his spirit could not make the journey to the land of the dead. The gods would be angry and take out their wrath on the people of Egypt.

The pharaoh's body had to be preserved. Then, it was sealed in a stone chamber and protected within the pyramid.

Life in early Egypt depended upon the Nile River. Egypt is a very dry country with endless sand dunes. The Nile provided water for crops, animals, and people.

The Egyptians believed that the land of the dead was west of the Nile. When the sun set in the west each day, they thought it traveled into the world where the gods and dead pharaohs lived. There are about 80 pyramids in Egypt, and all of them are built on the west bank of the Nile.

Most pyramids rest on a large, square base. The base of a big pyramid is several city blocks across. Each side is a perfect triangle.

We don't know why the early Egyptians built in the pyramid shape. The earliest Egyptian tombs were gravel burial mounds. The pyramids may have developed from the shape of these mounds. Perhaps the Egyptians thought the sloping sides of the pyramid were like a stairway to the sun on the journey to the next world.

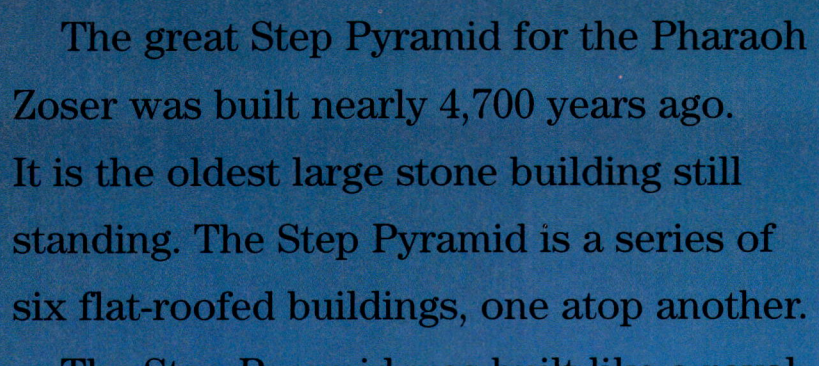

The great Step Pyramid for the Pharaoh Zoser was built nearly 4,700 years ago. It is the oldest large stone building still standing. The Step Pyramid is a series of six flat-roofed buildings, one atop another.

The Step Pyramid was built like a royal palace with many rooms. But there were no doors between the rooms because the pharaoh's spirit wouldn't need them in the next world.

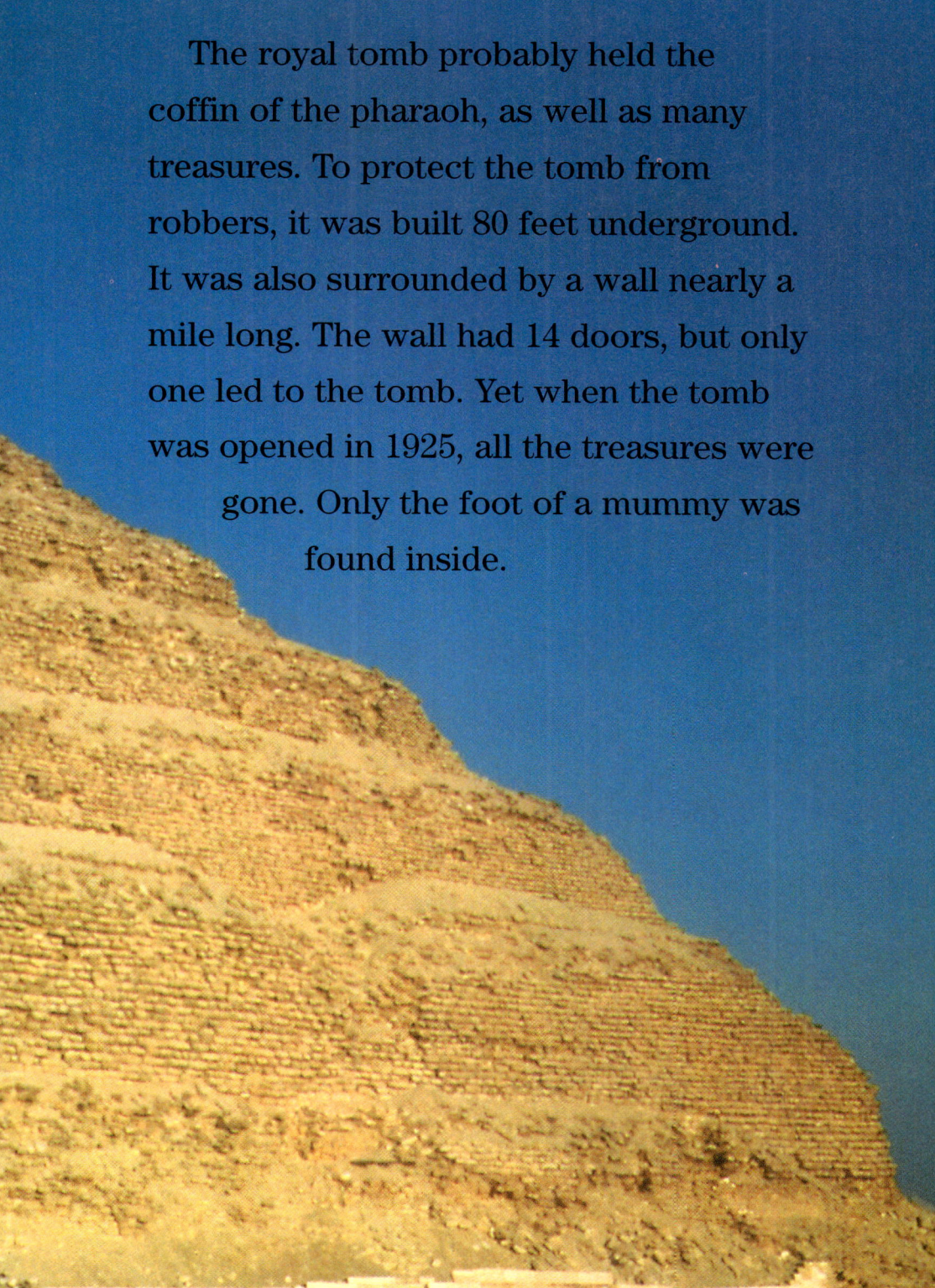

The royal tomb probably held the coffin of the pharaoh, as well as many treasures. To protect the tomb from robbers, it was built 80 feet underground. It was also surrounded by a wall nearly a mile long. The wall had 14 doors, but only one led to the tomb. Yet when the tomb was opened in 1925, all the treasures were gone. Only the foot of a mummy was found inside.

The Step Pyramid is surrounded by large courtyards and stone buildings carved out of solid stone with fake doors. We are not sure why. Perhaps the Egyptians thought the pharaoh could use them in the next world as if they were ordinary buildings. Or perhaps the solid buildings were a way of fooling grave robbers.

A life-sized statue of Pharaoh
Zoser was found in a closed room
in the pyramid. He is wearing a
special headcloth that is the sign
of royalty. His eyes, once inlaid with
rock crystal, were stolen from the
statue. But you can still see his fierce
expression, even after 4,700 years.

More than 4,500 years ago, three giant pyramids were built in Giza. Until the Eiffel Tower was built in 1887, the Great Pyramid of Pharaoh Khufu (KOO-foo) was the tallest building in the world. It rises 480 feet in the air, as tall as a 40-story skyscraper.

The square base is 756 feet on each side. That's about as big as seven city blocks. There are over 2 million stones in this pyramid. Amazingly, it probably took less than 30 years to build the entire pyramid.

When they were first built, the pyramids were covered in brilliant white limestone rock. The limestone has long since been stolen or destroyed.

The next largest pyramid was built 70 years later for Pharaoh Khafre (KAH-freh). It is ten feet shorter than the Great Pyramid of Pharaoh Khufu, but it looks taller because it was built on higher ground. The smallest pyramid, which was built for Pharaoh Menkaure (MEN-ka-ray), was the last one. It is 217 feet high.

Around the pyramids of Giza are rows of stone tombs for the members of the pharaohs' families and important court officials.

There are also smaller pyramids for Menkaure's three queens.

A larger-than-life-sized stone statue of Pharaoh Khafre was found near the pyramids. He is shown sitting on a lion throne. The falcon on the back of the throne represents Horus, the god who gave the pharaoh his strength and power.

After death, boats were provided for the pharaohs to use in the next world. In 1954, a boat pit was found just south of the Great Pyramid. It had been sealed by large blocks of limestone for over 4,500 years. Under the blocks were hundreds of pieces of carved wood. They were assembled into a boat larger than three school buses end to end.

The pharaohs' names were carved in oval or oblong figures called cartouches (car-TOOSH-ez). The names were in hieroglyphics (hi-row-GLIF-icks), the picture language that the ancient Egyptians used for writing. No one has written in hieroglyphics for 2,000 years. So we only can guess at the meanings of some of these pictures.

For 4,500 years, the statue of the Sphinx (SFINKS) has stood outside the Pyramid of Khafre. The Sphinx was carved from a huge outcrop of limestone. It is about 200 feet long and 65 feet high.

For centuries, the Sphinx was buried up to its neck beneath the drifting sands of the desert. Many attempts were made to clear it, but it was not dug out until 1925. It had been well preserved under the sand. But since it was uncovered, wind and air pollution are making it crumble.

The Sphinx has the body of a lion and the head of a pharaoh. Because lions are fearsome beasts, their statues were often used at the entrances to temples. The Sphinx was probably meant to guard the Pyramid of Khafre.

It took 70 days to prepare a pharaoh's body for burial. The process of preserving a body is called embalming.

First, the organs had to be removed from the body. Pieces of the brain were drawn out through the nostrils with an iron hook. The lungs, liver, stomach, and intestines were removed through a slit in

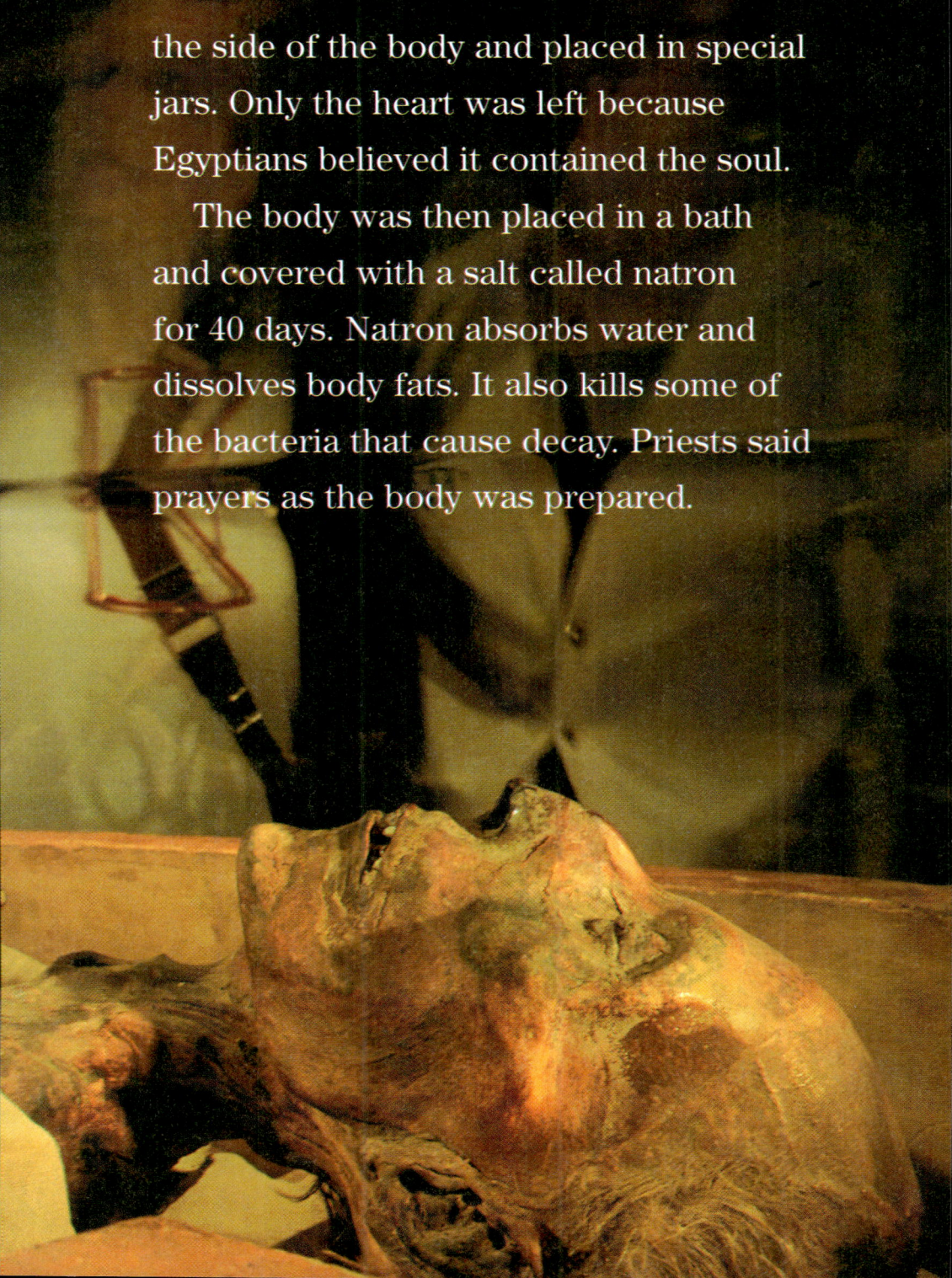

the side of the body and placed in special jars. Only the heart was left because Egyptians believed it contained the soul.

The body was then placed in a bath and covered with a salt called natron for 40 days. Natron absorbs water and dissolves body fats. It also kills some of the bacteria that cause decay. Priests said prayers as the body was prepared.

After 40 days, the body was washed and rubbed with oils and spices. The inside was stuffed with wads of natron and sand wrapped in linen. The face was painted and the hair neatly arranged.

A special hot wax was poured over the body. After it cooled and hardened, the skin was rubbed again with oil, wax, and spices.

The whole body was wrapped in linen bandages that had been soaked in the waxy material. Fingers, toes, arms, and legs were wrapped separately and then bound together. This process took about 30 more days. The mummy was then placed in a coffin called a sarcophagus (sar-KOF-eh-gus).

The pharaoh's sarcophagus was placed in a burial chamber somewhere beneath all the rocks. Gold and jewelry were buried with him.

To stop the tombs from being opened, the entrances to the chamber were sealed with huge blocks of stone. But despite the best efforts of the builders, almost every burial chamber found has had its contents plundered.

The only chamber ever found untouched was the underground tomb of Tutankhamen (toot-on-KAH-men), also known as King Tut. He was lying inside three coffins, one of which was solid gold. Nearly 3,500 treasures were buried alongside his body.

Pyramids were carefully planned before they were built. A site had to be found that was large and solid enough to support the enormous weight of the pyramid. It had to be on the west bank of the Nile and near enough that the stones could arrive by boat.

To make the site flat, the builders dug ditches on the site, filled them with water, and marked the water level. Then they hacked away all the rock above the level until the ground was completely flat. The southeast corner of the Great Pyramid is three football fields away from the opposite corner. Yet it is only one-half inch higher, smaller than your little finger.

Pyramids were built so that the sides are lined up due north, south, east, and west.

The pyramids were built mainly of limestone. Most of the blocks were cut from the ground near the building site, but special limestone and granite for the burial chambers came by boat from hundreds of miles away.

Using only copper chisels and wooden hammers, the workers slowly carved the stone blocks. With rods and strings they checked that the sides were cut straight. Smooth stones were used to polish the blocks so well that, legend has it, you could see your reflection. The blocks in the Great Pyramid fit together so tightly that you couldn't slip a knife between them.

The stones that make up the Great Pyramid weigh a total of about 6.5 million tons. Each block weighs an average of 5,000 pounds. But the biggest slab of rock in the roof of the pharaoh's chamber weighs 50 tons. That's as heavy as ten large elephants.

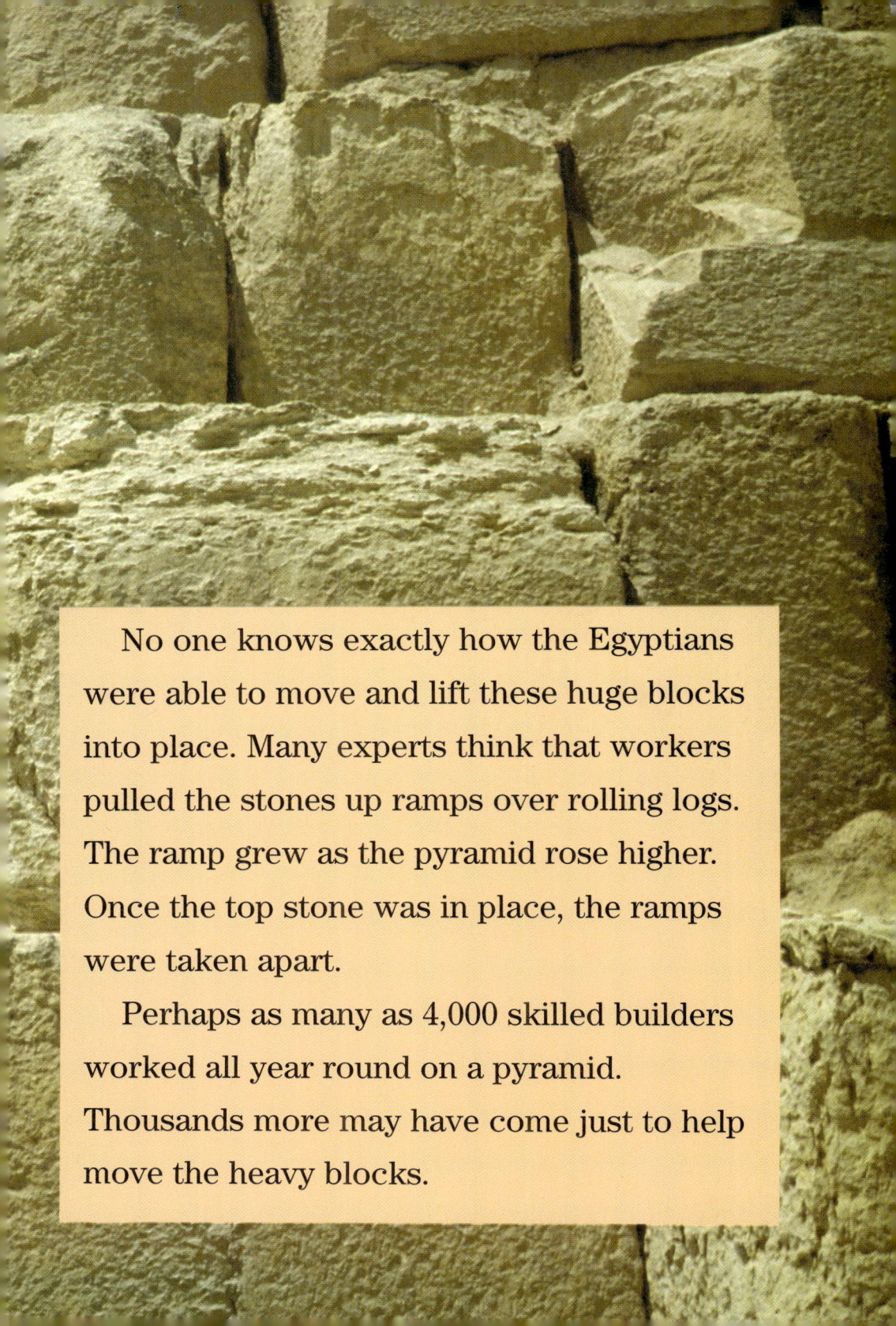

No one knows exactly how the Egyptians were able to move and lift these huge blocks into place. Many experts think that workers pulled the stones up ramps over rolling logs. The ramp grew as the pyramid rose higher. Once the top stone was in place, the ramps were taken apart.

Perhaps as many as 4,000 skilled builders worked all year round on a pyramid. Thousands more may have come just to help move the heavy blocks.

Nearly 2,000 years after the Egyptians, the Aztec and Mayan peoples of Mexico and Central America built pyramids as temples to worship their gods. These pyramids have flat tops and staircases on at least one side. Priests climbed the stairs to high altars where they conducted human sacrifices.

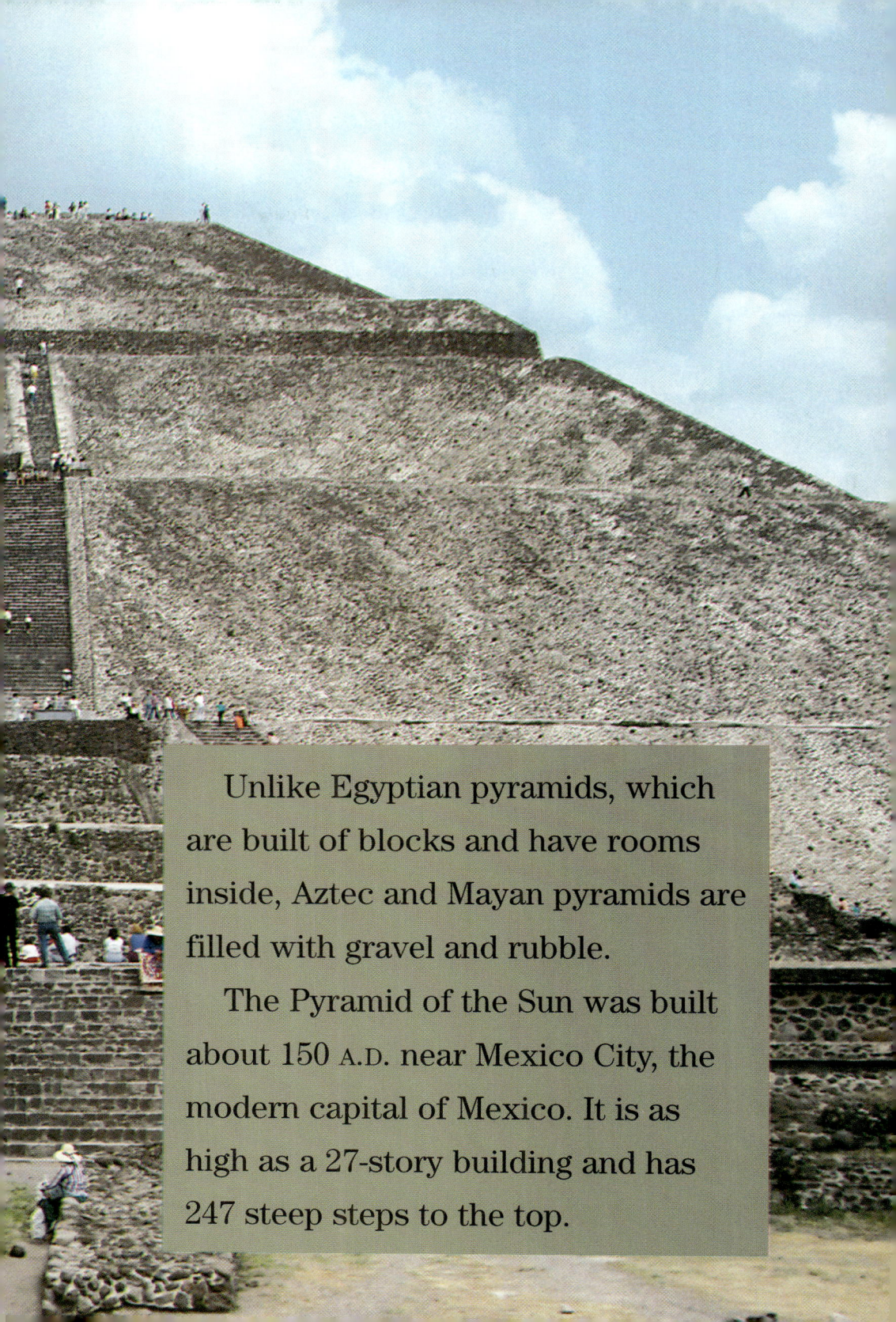

Unlike Egyptian pyramids, which are built of blocks and have rooms inside, Aztec and Mayan pyramids are filled with gravel and rubble.

The Pyramid of the Sun was built about 150 A.D. near Mexico City, the modern capital of Mexico. It is as high as a 27-story building and has 247 steep steps to the top.

Between the third and ninth centuries A.D., the Mayans built thousands of pyramids throughout southern Mexico and Central America. Hundreds were discovered only in the last century. Many more are still hidden in the dense rain forests of the area. Some of these pyramids had oval bases.

The El Castillo (el kus-DEE-oh) Pyramid in the ancient city Chichen Itza (cheet-zen-EET-zah) in southern Mexico has four staircases, three with 91 steps and one with 92 steps. That makes a total of 365 steps, one for each day of the year.

In modern times, new buildings have been built in the pyramid shape. In San Francisco, the Transamerica pyramid is designed to withstand earthquakes. Instead of stone blocks, it is built of steel and glass. The tip is 853 feet high, almost twice the height of the Great Pyramid.

In Las Vegas, a 36-story, pyramid-shaped hotel called the Luxor has elevators that travel up the slanting sides. In front of the hotel's parking lot is a ten-story copy of the Sphinx.

The pyramids of Egypt have
lasted for almost 5,000 years. No
other buildings on earth have lasted for
so long. But we are still learning new things
about the pyramids and the people who built them.